A Confluence of Voices Revisited

John Laue

FUTURECYCLE PRESS
www.futurecycle.org

Cover photo by Joshua Köller; author photo by himself; cover and interior book design by Diane Kistner; Gill Sans text with Alternate Gothic titling

Library of Congress Control Number: 2019935374

Published by FutureCycle Press
Athens, GA, USA

ISBN 978-1-942371-66-3

I dedicate this book to all the wonderful poets I've read, met, followed, edited, and loved in my eighty-two years of life— and to all my fellows with psychiatric struggles who may recognize states of mind described here.

May you pierce your crazy bubbles and come out the other side.

—Joel Mobius

Contents

"We are now in the age of Oprah, the age of non-fiction. We have a great hunger for what we think of as sincere revelation of a coherent self."

—Ellen Bryant Voigt, Interview
in the Missouri Review)

"The more poets are able to give a home to what is contradictory, ambiguous, and unruly, the more I would trust their sincerity, if by sincerity we also mean fidelity to the complexities of experience."

—Stephen Dunn, Walking Light

"I contain multitudes."

—Walt Whitman, Leaves of Grass

Tom Tenderfoot

Call it a wave, a rift, a space,
a height, a weight.

Call it a fluid, a gas, a size,
a particular shape.

Then close your eyes and change it
into what you want
to have, or be, or see.

Make it a woman's warmth,
a towering truth, an audible tree.

Then let it be.

Goliath Speaks

I thought he would be huge
as if carved from sun
with a voice of brass gongs,

that my veins might burst
and my heart echo
like a warning drum.

I thought that when he came
there would be silence,
eyes glancing back and forth,

that I would feel humble
in his presence,
even have the urge to run:

most of all that I
would see him as an enemy,
not a son!

Dana B. Fawn

When I was a child I cried once,
once only. I was like a vial of silences,
they tell me (I cannot recall).

It was when we studied Darwin,
not the brontosaurus or stegosaurus
or the bad tyrannosaurus rex:

I put them in my vial of silences,
as a good child would,
along with fairy tales and sex.

But later, when we studied Darwin
and the microscope,
I cried from awe, not fear.

I bent in two
and cupped my hands to catch
the tiny animals in every tear.

Petra Possible, Survivor

When the slant sun disappeared
and, high in the murk of dripping caves,
bats unclamped their claws
and dropped to shrill sonorities,
strange shapes came shadowing down,
launched in the night by fear.

Slight winds were snares in our ears.
We stopped and listened, ribs gone tight.
Whipped by their racing-horse heart,
each in the icy moonlight waited
for her own calamity, its figure silhouetted
like a man's, but larger, darker—

We waited there and nothing came but morning.
Then out of a glare of flat and total blue
it popped, impersonal as a clock.
And we were mercifully unprepared—

Annett Loveless

Stiff and dripping, with the arcs of waves
connecting all around his feet, he lay,
a heavy bird, a gull with hollow eyes,
this man who had let his manhood fall away.

The triple angles of his melting wings
recalled the times we stood like wooden piles
and watched him as he flirted with the sun,
his haloed body visible for miles.

But what was he, a man or just a bird?
We found him too long fallen from the skies
to resurrect him in his former stance
except upon the altars of our memories.

We let him lie beside the ramping waves
where infantries of sand birds would provide
a funeral with military honors,
a quick-time service ended by the tide.

Corporal Tim Washington

If I could be alive like fire,
O full of energy,
consuming everything that came my way,
I would grow and grow
till I lit the sky
and looked like cities in the night
to people traveling by.

If I could be like flame, like flame,
O done with pain,
treating everything the same,
I would burn my uniforms,
jump to Spain,
France, Switzerland,
and never bother to explain.

I would light upon a hill
above a lake,
dwell above the slow, still ripples
like a fiery fern.
And if they came
to turn me into shells,
I would leap into that lake
and never kill.

O never burn for them
and feed their hells!

Herb Mindfree, M.D.

The ultimate beasts are not out in the air
but in the mind; of this we are aware
who have seen the many-headed kind
through the backward stare of dreams
or have cut to the core of screams
through a tough and rubbery cortex rind.

Yet those that can break our brains like bread
have neither fangs nor ten-foot spread;
they are the simple shapes of humans,
eyes clenched in pain, fingers into fists.
They are our lists of walking wounded,
dead and dying, friends we kissed.

Quincy Collander

Sometimes, sitting at the tops of cities,
I have felt the sun reach out for me.
The sun, the central spark, heart of my universe;
and me, a taker of small gifts, a part of things.
I have felt a life within me stir
so small at first I could not trace its rise,
then larger, growing till it filled my senses.
And I have fled in fear from empty tops of buildings,
scrambled for the stairwell thinking I was ill.
But it grew each time, a life inside,
a little life that liked the sun.
It still grows. And it will.

Harvey Stonecypher

I will be inconspicuous
as silence on the desert,
blameless as a breeze;
I will wear green when hunting,
           brown when riding,
           blue when swimming;
and when you come to see me I
shall not be there.

I will be impeccable
to microscopic eyes,
cautious as a thief.
I will follow the crowed,
           move as they move,
           do as they do;
so when you come to see me I
shall not be there.

Only my shadow will know you;
only my image will speak.
When you look in my eyes
you will see a disguise,
           two zeros of lies,
           your self-same surprise,
that when you come to see me
I shall not be there.

Grandma May Amoro

You say we do not understand your love?
Once when we were young
we gave ourselves for valentines,
redeemed ourselves by touch and breath.
We were traditional lovers
kissing the soft parts,
careful with the moisture of each other.
We might have been figures
etched upon a goblet,
seen with *vino rosso*
upon the table of a Roman senator.
We would have made the same parentheses
upon a sheeted page
as Daphne and Apollo, Troilus and Cressida,
many of the classic lovers.
But in the end we found
that it was all a game
that had been played before and won,
the athletes, recovered, sitting round
to laugh at us, still running.
After all, we found
we loved by merely living.

H. Howard Hexagon

I pity those poor poets
who say that love will save us
from this detonating world.
I pity them and yet admire them too:
they have the innocence of children
spinning in dream orbits,
walking naked in the light of day.
They see the stars in angry afternoons,
and above them always
looms one little ray of hope.

I have seen the corners
where they spoke; the people staring
vacant-eyed as calves,
ready to be led
to new, ridiculous extravagances.
They teach that the meek will win,
and yet it is always the meek
who fall beneath the tide
or crouch, afraid, in corners
and are crushed to dust
when governments collide.

I pity them, poor pale idealists,
so wrapped in their sweet innocence
they think that justice will prevail.
They fail to realize
the strong are favored,
and they often aren't the just.
Only searching all the world for hate,
hating hate, and fighting it with fire
will keep safe all of us.

Jack Root

Put this also in your letterbox:
I thought you had forgotten those eyes
that watched from the goat-bearded moon;

I thought you could look up in peace
and not see luminous crosses in the sky
or other visions of His potency.

When we were engaged, I believed
that we could vary the routine,
try such frictions as would kindle more.

But I was tampering with your faith.
I did not know you got your gifts by grace
and only so. I had no means to know.

You should have told me of the jealousy
of that heavenly shape of love before
you stamped this image as if on a coin:

you of subtle, conjugal promise
kneeling in the bedroom of your shame,
waiting for a star to touch you like a wand.

Robert Bitterroot

When my mother, with her wet cramp,
laid me in a puddle on the sheet,
I felt like a goldfish spilled from the bowl,
for it was cry or die;
                    and how many heartbeats had I?

But I recovered, swam like a minnow
unto the shallow shoals. In my frank
and friendly way I kissed the world,
for it was this or die;
                    and how many heartbeats had I?

Later and larger, I cut like a shark
through the schools of circumstance, chewed
the hands that fed me straight into their hearts;
for it was eat or die;
                    and how many heartbeats had I?

Then, independent, smart as a whale,
I slipped all grappling hooks.
I look at the dark of a kelpless deep,
for it was dive or die;
                    and how many heartbeats had I?

Randy Woods

Many times I have tried to open myself,
to let the cougar of the sun come into me
and stalk, majestic, through my shadowed corridors.
Sometimes, drowsing on a public lawn,
I feel the footsteps in my veins
and arch my back to catch the gathering warmth,
curve my neck to hold the heavy head.

I dream of widening circles of the sun
till the grass around me turns to ash,
and in museums sheets of glass fold down
to run in rivulets along the halls.
I see the padded beasts displayed there now,
twitching, stepping off their pedestals,
waiting with unwavering patience for the rains.

J. P. Grady

Tic-tac-toe and the little typist
taps the letters out
across the screen in strips.

It makes me pause in awe
the way her hands caress
the clean cool eyes of the machine

like a blind girl reading Braille,
or perhaps a nun with beads,
such concentration painted on her face.

I can almost see the neural arcs,
the sparks that ripple down white arms
to fingertips initialed with the keys.

I wonder if her hands still twitch
in sleep, if her dreams drum on the sheet
like music from piano rolls.

I want to set her free,
to push her gently off the page
and into the grand impulsive life.

But she taps on and on,
rehearses reflex of a million words
and millions more to come.

I hover near her, dumb,
but convinced I will have to dance
to the rhythms of this typist.

Don J. Duquesne

(After seeing "La Strada")

Step right up here, ladies.
Bring your chains.
Step up. I'm the original man.
This rib might be
a relative to one of yours.
Step right up here,
sweating in the hot sun,
and I will place the chains so,
around my chest.
Note the expansion,
the perfection of the torso.
And let me tell you
of the enormous lungs,
which wait like wings
to open at your order.
Move in closer;
get a better look.
Put your delicate hands
up to my chest
and feel this heart
that beats a bouncing ball
against your palms.
Put the tight links
of your arms here, ladies.
Think of the sun,
that hot sweet apple sun
that beats upon your belly,
warms you to the bone.

Now hold it for a minute.
Fold me in your body.
Follow my directions.

                    (next please)

Come!

Juan Martinez, Orchardist

(At the burning of his apple grove)

Listen how the green wood spits and hisses,
seethes and sizzles in the flame
like burning flesh,
like men among the snakes of flame.
O Lord, the fire is spelling out our names.

My Lord, remember when the world was young;
no stain was on us then.
We were so proud
to share a meal with such a flickering tongue.
And O the pain, the pain that we were wrong.

Now look at our faces, shrunken, seared,
for we were cut off from our growth.
The only truth we know:
dry lips across a hollow tooth.
Lord, we are still sour from drunken youth.

O Mary, give us hope for we are burning.
All our lives are turning in this fire.
Our knees are bent
and we are blinded by the light.
O Lord, the fire is beckoning tonight.

Hail Mary, how the green wood hisses.
Smoke mocks our movements with its kisses.
We see sparks
instead of stars above the chapel.
How the apple burns, the apple turns, the apple—

Dale Tryst

When I think of death
I think of the separate veins,
their blood congealing;
the slow flood stopped
across the heart;
the tendons of the thighs,
each rigid, standing out
as if a final climax came.
I think of the tips of fingers
when the tiny ridges stiffen, tingling,
at the last emphatic pulse;
how the eyes must dim,
come on again, and dim
as if a surf washed over them.
And then the final towering wall
of water, tilting into darkness,
the slide headfirst as in
a foundering ship down miles of dark
from one slow-motion arc into another,
till, at last, the perfect silence
of the bottom reels you in.
You are sure you are at rest.
And then, perhaps, your death begins:
a slow and careful sealing.

Professor Peavy and the Motorcyclists

I hear their engines hammering at the night again.
Surely they must be fools,
these hunchbacked, leather-heavy men
who fly so close to the ground,
diving down asphalt hills a foot from death,
all goggled and strapped and visored,
half-raptor, half-machine,
and always, always seeking greater force
from the union of flesh and steel.

They must be completely mad
to stretch the limits of their risks so far;
surely insane, entirely bastardized,
feet grown fast to metal of accelerators,
blood sprayed into chambers and ignited,
brains ruled by reflex of exploding pistons.
I dismiss them. *Fools!* I cry into the night
when they send their nets of light across the wall
and I lie awake and dream of white-hot speeds.

Jared Gentle

Slowly, with the weight of many centuries upon them,
old wheels turn along the rutted ground.
And I, who have never heard this sound,
somehow know it now: strange squeak of wheels
set into axles by a peg, the suck of mud
at feet of oxen, the rattle and the strain of wood.
I hear it now, as I can hear the sounds
of wars for many centuries, and see disasters grow
from flash of swords to brief and terrible suns.
The filaments of men's minds glow brightly
over near horizons, and I pause to listen,
counting seconds to the slow, inexorable sound.
But what I hear while waiting for man's thunder
are the distances of history: peasants felling trees
and sawing them in sections, women beating hides,
and children crying awe at the immensity—
great wooden wheels to ride over rutted ground.

Anna Anselm Arthur

(After a lumberman said the members
of the Sierra Club were "possessed by poets")

Is it because I come possessed by poets
to these redwoods' tall cathedrals
that I walk so softly here?

Some men would not react this way;
conscious of their trades,
they would be estimating board feet.

Already in the distance I can hear
the hungry shriek of saws
as lumber barons spread their territories southward.

Yet these majestic, vertical presences entrance me,
turn my thinking to the past,
to what earth was and what it has become.

I walk and wonder of two thousand years
and what these trees have seen of history
while red burls shine like ancient eyes.

Now closer, to my left, a new saw starts.
The rings of many centuries burn inward.
A sound like murder dominates the air.

Is it because I come as poet
that the saws' wails echo for me
after the actual sounds trail off?

I turn to leave as axes clink on wedges.
The hard blows penetrate my skull,
lodge sharp splinters in my heart.

Lucy Lee

I was far behind him
yet saw twin beams of light
ascend the evening sky,
too quick for searchlights,
then complete their sweep.

When I reached the curve
his blood was on the ground
and they were there,
that sudden circle that appears
when death is near.

I did not need
to wonder who they were:
I had seen them once before
when I lay bleeding
on the broken ground.

I watched them closely,
faces of the curious,
intent and incomplete,
with a kind of longing
showing in the depths of eyes.

They first appeared reluctant
yet soon pressed over him,
fighting for their need
to breathe his breath
and cut him from the sky.

I stood behind them thinking,
if that man should be alive
and stir and, blurry-eyed, look up,
he will always recognize
the composite face of death.

August Auger

Shall we celebrate the dawn
when harps and pillars of light
slope down waterfalls,
pink the eyes of animals
that twitch in their morning sleep?

When on grass blade arches
beetles' backs begin to glow
and the ground-low inchworms
hump and butt their heads?

When snakes in their holes uncoil
and swivel out to catch the sun,
their sharp tongues fluttering,
the glisten of their scales a treasure chest?

When at the roots of rivers,
where the shore is stamped with stories,
beavers drag long liquid Vs,
pulling the streams behind them?

Shall we celebrate the dawn
when tongues of light
knife through curtains' laces,
rise chest-high on walls
of dark-dimensioned rooms
like golden calendars unfurling?

O look at us now, the human race:
a pale girl starts and blinks
at the shrill of rainbows in her face;
a naked boy recoils
as his wakened sneeze
roils a universe of sunlit dust.

Today is Monday: it is six a.m.
We must brush sleep-webs away,
pry the matter from our lids,
and walk erect with the sun
above our heads like some great halo.

But today we fail to celebrate
as animals may, in glad awakening.
Sleeping late, we stir reluctantly,
think of burgeoning wars,
tension stretched to crises,
centuries of bitterness
building to a head.

No wonder we turn in our beds,
pull the covers tight,
curl their spines, hide in the heat
that rises from our thighs.
Soon toxic dust
may coat our pillows.

We could watch our world
be overwhelmed by waste
till we fall into such deep shadows
naked eyes are useless
frozen globes of glass.

We could see our hallowed greatness
fade to smoking ruins
as dawn's low animals
race for their holes
while devastation's robot angels pass.

Tara Darwish

As the wren, by instinct,
flies south across the quickening air,
so did she sing when winter came
of wet winds, heavy with crystal,
bending boards of barns,
torched icicles in sunlit eaves,
snow-holes poked by water.
She was frost's glad caller:
the woolly whistle of her breath
sent plumes of celebration
into doveless trees,
their branches wet as lust,
their bases knuckled, clenched.

Spruces in loud storms' vibratos
loosed their sagging loads,
saluting her as she trod along,
left footprint signatures
on snow-white, shining fields.
Bridges, heavy with new ice,
creaked with pressure
as she trod their frozen paths.
Ponds whose thin, quicksilver skin
would not have held a bird
supported her as she picked her way.
Even wolves appeared to favor her.

She often stood long minutes
still as a snowman listening
to drips of water from bare trees.
Then in a sober, mystical mood
she crossed the ice-bound brook
that whispered past her home,

entered the old Victorian house,
and wiped the sweating windows clean.
From there she watched
the evenings tilt away.
As shadows clotted on the fields
impressions of that world
poured from her fertile pen.

She was winter's chosen poet,
bard of hip-deep drifts. I knew her
only through blurred visions,
but she gifted me that season
with bright, sparkling odes.
Then, when the sun stood up,
snow ebbed with the moon;
the days grew longer, lighter.
I called on her again
for more short luminous lines,
but she refused to answer.
Without a word or wave goodbye,
she vanished into nature's wilds,
my fever's dreamsong sprite.

Jonathon Northcutt, Able Seaman

Could this harsh hulk of a man
have been our captain?
It was a year's astonishment
to all of us who stared
at the clamped eyes
and the thunderous mouth betrayed
by the deepest silence time could muster.

Surely this was a mirage,
for he was strange and twisted
as if seen by illusion of bent light
through fathoms of dark water.
We saw, not him,
but a shipwrecked shape
lying on its back in an old room
open to the currents;
and we were only tourists,
gawkers from glass-bottomed boats,
below us surface tension never broken.

Long ago we had known him differently,
when, proud in the brass of command,
he had paced the bridge,
his hands behind him,
gripping every now and then
his visionary lenses.
In his calm and distant gaze
was a knowledge of sea problems,
a solid understanding of horizons
echoed by the levels of his eyes.

With no miss or hurry in his pacing,
he would drop calm commands
into the tube, casual it seemed,

yet we knew his rectitude
to be that of an angel.
We, down below, decked in shadow,
would obey him,
running from ladder to hold,
stoking, scrubbing,
filled with a sense of utility.

So at the altar of our captain
we worshipped by efficiency.
And through it all he stood
with the sun at his head,
a dazzling image, vision of trust,
alone on the bridge. Even at night,
when the glow from his pipe
caught his features in a weird, red radiance,
we looked up and were comforted.

We rode on an island of belief,
bearing our tonnages back and forth
across the faceless sea,
and the waves did not scare us,
or the winds, or the slam of the surf,
or the low and lonely foghorns.

There was that night off Madagascar
when the typhoon came
and the loud waves crossed our stack.
It seemed that the whole world
was a trough of depths
in the moody mountains of those waves,
yet we rode it out,
shaved our faces in the morning.

There were the days of Arctic cold
when we swerved past icebergs like a fish,
never touching with our hull,

twisting, turning
past the great spread fingers that awaited us.
The captain did not blink
at the frost that rimmed his eyes
but kept watch, calmly ordered us on.

So we rode through twenty years of chaos
safely in our faith,
and the flags never waved
a doubt along the wind,
nor the radio beacon tapped
a single signal of distress.

And then that fog came;
thick as a dream it billowed about us,
closed the captain from our sight.
We could not see the funnel
or the waves against the hull,
only knew by the sound
that we were making progress:
the old ship throbbed with the life
of her engines, more conspicuous now
for the lack of sight.

We slid along, lost in the foghorn's blasts,
for what seemed like hours.
Then it came: an altered instant
when astonishment stopped time.
We heard accordions of metal
and the unceasing fold of ribs.
We were thrown off our feet,
scattered and bashed like pool balls
caroming off the bulkheads.

We felt her listing to starboard
as the engines turned into reverse,
but it was too late: the great ship
buckled, foundered like a whale.

There was a loud explosion,
and we thought she wanted to sound.
No order to abandon came,
but we seven ran for the pulleys, panicked.

———

It was evening and the fog was lifting.
We watched her burn
from the only boat we thought had launched.
The long light reached across the water
like a fiery finger echoed in each guilty eye.
Soon the stern hove up; she shuddered
into the broad suck of a whirlpool, steaming,
wreckage turning round and round.
In our minds we could see
the torn hull falling, spinning though dark water,
through the perfect stillness of the currents,
after hours and days still falling,
rocking like a leaf—

———

Each of us went our separate ways
when we were rescued.
After the board of inquiry
where in perjury our stories matched,
Old Hanrahan, the superstitious Irishman,
decided for the Emerald Isle;
White went to Wales to see his family;
Norden shipped on a freighter going to Formosa;
Brandenburg stayed home,
started the garden he had always talked about.

Yet we kept in touch:
the letters with far postmarks crossed meridians,
filled the seamen's box in Boston.
Some of us were near when the article ran
and came to see—

a body identified as that of Captain Calvin S. Noble,
Master of Ships, presumed lost when his craft
"The Good Hope" sank off the coast of Newfoundland
five years ago, July 12, 1934.

Could this wretched wreck have been
the man we so admired?
Here, in a chapel filled with incense,
lying, candles around his head
and the coffin flowers oozing from their cuts?
We were dumbstruck by the question.
Drake, the first mate, glanced at me
and moved his lips as if to say,
These remains could never be our captain's;
he stayed with the ship just as he should,
went down so deep no one could raise him.
I have seen his face beneath the waves
and heard the still-suspended bell
toll out an alls-well-six
ever so faintly from the bottom!

Peter Paul Persimian

He appears mad indeed but to a few, because the majority
is infected with the same disease. —Horace, 64 BC

(The Myth)

Let there be light,
He said, and an ape echoed Him,
gesticulated like a puppet, shuffled,
made his mean way through a maze of abstract ferns,
holding his new-stalked thumbs gingerly as he lurched along.
And very soon he climbed, this oscillating ape,
to the highest peak of the grandest tree
and, swaying there precariously,
beat his staccato chest
and claimed it:

All of it,
all the light,
the cold and incoherent darkness,
animals, fish, birds reptiles, insects,
the multiple plant-forms in their green and virile fountainings;
all the waters: oceans, lakes and ponds;
the hardened granites jutting from new landscapes;
the massed grandeur and sculptured silences
of mountains, seamed valleys,
bush-eyed prairies.

And he also claimed ideas:
this ape, who had gradually grown a tongue,
became metaphysical, began to contemplate
his apeness. While other animals grazed, he gazed
into natural mirrors, fancied himself quite handsome, noble even.
He also found, in the essence of himself,
two poles like those of the tortured earth

that wrenched at his togetherness,
drove him to lay in provisions
of proverbs, laws, gods.

Since the beginning,
when the original tear-shaped cave
was hung with the furry triangles of bats
and the long-armed figures squatted on their haunches,
cold in a blood-red dawn, the tension of the poles has drawn him
to a choice: either the hunting reflex, shooting rapid nerves,
or the god-like rule that thought can offer
a glimmer of fire. The totem
of his spine is multiple,
both man and animal.

(The Problem)

To know who we are—
mumbled the young philosopher,
scratching his back against a banyan tree.
Knowing is like following a shell's strange spiral,
diving deeper down the circular staircase of the mind's immensity,
growing dizzy. Yet it is there, in that strange density,
the inner core reveals true meanings:
visions come and light the walls;
as in a powerful acid bath,
we're permanently etched.

I know what I was.
I've seen cave pictures on the walls,
old animals, their portraits drawn in blood.
Once, in a dream, I saw them flicker into motion, rise
to a tail-whipped, muscle-rippled silence, searching, scanning
for the lost prey and its succulent meat.
I was the artist who froze them there
in ape-ecstatic marks.

I was a hunter
of the hunters.

But what have I become
in this "enlightened" circle—
desk-sitter, presser of switches, pale obsessor,
content with a glimpse of animals I knew so well,
never to see, except in dreams, that action I still crave?
Perhaps it was this that made my mother mad, made her whistle
matrons through dim corridors, wrestle light and dark beliefs,
fight invisible beasts called alpha, beta, gamma—
No matter now. She sleeps in a time
before the legendary dawn of harps—

But I live on
like an overslept guest now awake
and entranced by the simian shapes of men.
When they gaze at the sky, their faces seem blunt
with an old desire. The bear, the wolf, the tantalizing lion
stalk across that starry front. If we could claim
the poles those lights print on our eyes,
would we grow whole and one?
And would it be as hunters,
hunting, or as the hunted?

Roger Reckoning

In South America, they say,
passions spring unconquered
from the silences.
Pools of shadow
drip with softened sap.
No human ear can hear
the spots that ripple there,
slip upon a branch to wait,
their glinting, slitted eyes
fixed on green alleyways.

In South America, they tell me,
last week's meals make hips
upon trapezed green snakes
who hang, already hungry,
under broad banana leaves
well camouflaged
by lily-livered vines.

They tell me that, in South America,
even the quietest waters
breed disaster, flash and ripple,
break and close on hunter and prey,
leaving only vague red stains
that swirl a moment
like accelerated flowers,
then sink out of sight.

But how can I comprehend
who have never seen the jaguar strike,
or the awakened crocodile,
or snakes that drop their coils
like quoits
over an unwary walker?

It is inconceivable to me
(I have never been to jungles)
that in South America
they should not be like us,
mostly fearing people.

Beth Duncan

I moved the rock and there he was,
coiled snake, like an eye's bright retina
with its varicolored interstices.

For one sprung moment I was hung above him
even as he broke his pose and slithered off.
Then reflex leapt into my knees; I staggered back.

Later, when my blood abandoned its crescendo
and my heartbeat's bell of sound stopped ringing,
I could not cease obsessing on the snake.

And even now, though many months have passed,
I think of the one scared look we shared
and wonder if he still survives;

if somewhere in a root-lined hole,
my frightened image flashes through his colors,
accelerates his heart as he remembers.

Sam Slipper, Schizophrenic

*The pure products of America
go crazy—*

—William Carlos Williams

Like separate fires on a mountainside,
the rages burned within me.

Night came and I felt myself
a mass of glowing coals.

I fell asleep then, smoldering;
when I woke I was nothing but holes.

Jason Mason

To my new wife

Are you aware
you've wedded one of the dead?
I've walked the streets of hell
for years now,
shattered like dropped glass.

I've certain understandings
of reality: illusions they may be,
but they cause me to act differently
than most other men,
feel dangerous emotions,
see divergent messages
in ordinary landscapes.

You like me
because I'm gentle
and resemble your sister.
But what about my death?
How in the face of hell can I love you
like a sister, like a brother,
like an adequate husband?

Even when you imitate
the 1950s cheerleader
that you really were,
I cherish you.
Yet visions of witches,
demons, ghosts and goddesses
fill me so completely
I imagine my skull
as movie screen
or Plato's cave itself.

The ashes of my death are in me.
I can't be that husband
you fantasized about
when you were little.
But who can preserve
the illusions of childhood?
Certainly not I. Not even you.

You're more fortunate than some;
you've certain guarantees from me:
that I need you; yes, I need—
that I'll attempt to please,
try not to fool myself or you
with my delusions.

But I married you, you say,
so I should share your hopes,
fears, dreams and speculations—
And I think of the truth of this:
I was alone; so were you;
we chose to compromise
in a scenario
we both could comprehend.

It seemed better to choose you
than echoes from the grave,
although I love them too—sometimes
to distraction, I'm afraid.

Maybe burnt-out birds can fly.
Perhaps the Phoenix isn't myth
but lives in all the dead like a seed.

We make our limp, pathetic efforts;
friction seems to warm us.
Is it another of my illusions,
or do intact parts of the spirit appear
like bones, like buds, like nubs of wings—?

James Weatherstone, Madman

For years I carried around my brain
in bloody hands,
no skull enclosing it, or skin,
or even strands of hair—
like a naked embryo
torn out of the womb
without the placental waters
to protect it.

Unprepared even to suck mother's milk
I went, every breeze a hurricane
on the sensitive nerve endings,
emotions magnified a hundred times
as if shouted through bullhorns
by the Gestapo;
ideas, symbols, images intensified
till I couldn't tell them from reality.

I was lost in hidden meanings,
never knowing I'd imposed them on myself.
Yet I kept going
through the waking nightmare,
the dark of a terrible sun.
I'd wanted to understand,
to gain some vague, indefinable insight
into the birth and death of the soul.

Sometimes even the smallest concreteness eluded me
as the sound of the cricket shuts down
at the approach of larger animals.
The real and illusory mingled
in inextricable ties.
What before had been pleasurable

evaded me. Joy hid in grief
and hope was another grave.

I thought I'd found an alternate reality,
but the world transformed a thousand times a day
in its meanings and its intimations.
Nothing was stable: time, space,
structure of bodies, order of dimensions.
All the continuities I'd believed in gone,
changed, changed, in flux—
Instead, perfidious magical laws
were in effect, and even they were changing,
changing with the wind—

I performed strange rituals,
rites from the blood-drenched past,
did meaningless ablutions,
made signs into altered air,
scratched at the doors of friends
who wore ceremonial masks—
and the sacrifice was me; I knew it:
all of the knives were pointed at me;
the accidents were mine;
fire sirens were meant for me,
the haunted house, the Satanists—

When people called their dogs, I came.
Random conversations transformed my whole consciousness.
Attitudes of bodies, gestures of all kinds,
colors, scents, even street names, license plates
were dicta of the most profound importance.

And, having died already,
I made my plans to end for good.
I stored away pills and went to bridges,
cliffs and roofs and dared myself.

All that stopped me was curiosity
as to what new paths the agonies would take.

And, worst of all, I failed to gain;
or what I gained seemed minimal then.
It was all I could do to survive at the time.
But I don't regret it now
in the light of the ordinary world.
Or rather, I have but one regret:
that fear was my companion;
I was fear's kept man
for several terrible years.

Although the skull's now closed
around my brain,
the blood's been replaced,
and the nerves are tied up tight again
by medicine and my own guided hands,
at odd times, in the restroom,
by the filing cabinets,
or in the midst of chattering crowds,
I find myself silently shouting,

Dale, why did you reject me then,
when I was humble and obsessed with love,
when I had so little left to lose?

I served my mortal soul to you;
you turned it to a tattered shroud,
then scorned me as a fool.

His answer echoes in my mind,
a kind of crazy mockery:

You chose to be damned by choosing me.
We live with the hells we choose!

Leonard Slain's Egg

I

The man in the long black Cadillac
lights a match.
It flares in his face.
A communication happens.
I tail him through a maze of streets
turning and returning
till he enters a freeway
and I can't keep up.
Illumination speeds away.
A million secrets are unveiled
but I'm one of the blind, the ghosts
who ride with hollow sockets in their skulls
attempting to choose. But what?
The Mafia? The devil's eyes?
Assignations in hell?
And now, because I've thought of the Mafia,
I've a certain membership,
a ring that can't be broken
except by spiritual death.
Confused, I follow other cars,
red, white, green, blue, yellow,
each with significant numbers on its plate.
I wind through alleyways,
swinging in quick Us,
not wanting to commit myself
to any of their lives for very long.
This world's a paradox of contradictions
to be sorted only when I comprehend
the I Ching of pure chance—

II

O people in night cars, what gods you follow,
for how long, how you keep your lives in balance,
what you prefer to eat and drink,
all these are signified by colors,
symbols, signs. I assume you know them
since you bear your coded signatures
so neatly on your license plates,
since you signal me so discreetly.
What if I see a 007?
Should I follow the license to kill?
We were nothing in that other world
unless we could kill.

> They marched us out to a flat field,
> put us in lines facing each other.
> "You're either the quick or the dead!"
> they shouted from the tower.
> "Even-numbered lines will be first.
> Now growl! Vertical butt stroke! Growl!
> Lunge! And repeat after me,
> THE SPIRIT OF THE BAYONET'S TO KILL!"

I never wanted to take lives.
Killing was foreign to me
as dying for some other people.
Hell's Angels, the Mafia, the police, the Army,
all could kill. But I saved bees,
put poisonous spiders out the door.
And now I'd simply like to preserve my being,
find some slight stability,
discover harmonious ways
to penetrate the laws of chance.
Already I've not been the quick:
my consciousness floats naked as a baby's,

its accustomed body burnt to ashes
in that other distant world.
But I've found temporary shelter here,
clothed in a casing made in Germany
that I bought from a poet for $500.
Till I grow a new skin,
till my skull bones knit together
in this strange and alien place,
my spirit's safe
in one small vehicle
my fragile green steel egg—

Dan Dimagico

This must be another universe,
one of the alternate ones
not so tangible as that where I succumbed.
I'm a newborn ghost,
my awareness shifted to this body.
The feeling of weightlessness pervades me
as if I could float in air like smoke.
Here part of me has been living all along,
conducting a similar life with different rules
among the ghosts, the shadows that are real.
Glad my consciousness was transferred here,
that there's someplace after death,
I leave the orphanage and go out
to search for my rebirthing shape.
Shall it be as butterfly, plant,
animal or bird? Or human again?
I only know it will be planned but accidental.
How many other worlds I'll enter,
with what length of lives, what limitations
are now mysteries wrapped in starry nets
of universal consciousness.
But I've begun to cut through the confusion.
This must be how we evolve,
not backward or forward in time, but simultaneously.
Wind blows through me as I float along
barely feeling the pressure of my steps,
noticing small differences between this world
and the one I suddenly left.

Elegy for Skeptics

In most important matters,
the price of certainty is blindness.

Blake Reservoir, The Passing

Did death break like a wave
over his pillowed head?
Or did it come in tiny increments,
soft steps upon a stair?
They'd no way of knowing,
standing there like butlers
waiting for assignments.

He was dead and they were caught
in the midst of reveries,
amazed.

They'd expected a rattle
to come bubbling from his chest
or, lacking that, even the slightest tremor
signaling the end would have sufficed.

But there was nothing visible.
Only under the sealed and fevered lids
a certain little light slid from his eyes
and Harry left them poised above an empty space.

They leaned like parentheses
over the peaceful face.
Each wanted to speak
but there were no words,
only the sound of wind beating the curtains
over the windowsill.

Phillip Diamondcutter, Embalmer

At the town's tail end
Phil, the little embalmer,
hums a dirge-like ditty:
song of all the sharp things,
the coverings, the consummations,
the gentle and maniac violences,
the entrances, the exits,
the self-contained decays,
the local and general injuries,
the breakages and desecrations—
he's seen them all.

He sings of the precision of the carpenter:
Harry's casket is a masterpiece
of mortise-and-tenon accuracy,
its lid designed to fit the shadow perfectly.
Phil sings that everything is in its place
and, singing, he enjoys his art,
turns the body to a shell,
replaces all life's fluids with bitter wine.

We may envy him
for he sees meaning here:
death is his life.
Under a day-bright neon light,
his quick hands flicker in and out
with practiced grace;
his taxidermy shows the stroke of genius.

He's grown calm
since he came to his trade,
saw the blind and final shape
of each man's fate
spread before him on the table.

Fred Wallenstone, Mason

Some of our greatest art
is in remembrance of the dead,
remarks Fred O., the mason.
Think of the pyramids.
See where the planes of tombs
and mausoleums meet the wind
and gesture man's magnificence.

These monuments to human greatness stand
like silent, massive ships,
all sealed, all keeping in the darkness.

Yet at dawn, the tents of shadow stay
as definite as all our stone facades.
And in the afternoon, the shadows stretch
across the landscape, lengthening
till evening comes and leaves us small
and cautious in our blindness.

What frightened lines we sometimes speak,
thinking of man's magnificence
while huddled in our rooms,
eyes full of fearsome images,
hearts rattled by the wind—
we, the chosen people of dark shadows.

Arthur Scarbird, Philosopher

Art S., a philosopher of my acquaintance,
expounds on death:

We can't insult the figures in the coffins;
they've been carefully cared for,
rinsed out, purged, and pickled
till they're little more than simulacrums
of living flesh.

The bodies' owners wouldn't care
if we drew and quartered them,
pried their tendons from their bones,
stuck needles in their drying eyes.

It's for themselves
the preachers' fingers waggle by the grave,
the masons chisel cunning corners on the stones,
the carpenters grip the coffin nails
as if they were alive.

It's for themselves
the poets, long-faced in dim lamplight,
write of death.

Each provides his own distractions,
sends up small balloons of metaphor.

But the ball of shadow
in the corpse's open mouth
speaks louder.

Leonard Tremelo, Musician

For my funeral, ventures Lennie,
an aging virtuoso,
play a booming exorcism.

Let the drums rumble syncopated rhythms
and the flutes insinuate
above the innuendos of the clarinets.
Let the brass blare its whorish blare
and stare at the crowd with multiple eyes,
and give the triangle to a minister
to play three-cornered notes.
Might that be enough to wake the dead?

But even if our ancient mummies rose
in choirs of hallelujah,
winding bandages around a maypole
or singing praise to science,
would it matter much
except to make an overpopulated world?

Some would sermonize about it,
some hoist glasses at loud cocktail parties,
some play fateful games of chance.

But each would hear his own internal voices,
each his body's rhythms, slowing, speeding,
each his heart, his vulnerable heart,
which may hesitate in death's presence,
then race out like hoofbeats
of a startled deer.

Annette Purplethorn, Clergy

Reverend Anne, a local minister, declares
we'll have *La Vie Eternelle*:

It's God's will that for each there's a time
when life meets death:
the organs hang like cities
in the belly of the night
and wink out one by one;
the trains of the blood grow silent;
death hunkers on the cooling tracks.
But the soul!—The soul does rise
like a newly loosed balloon.

Perhaps we should have faith,
but darkness shuffles overhead,
confusing as a pack of cards
in a black magician's hands,
and we begin our questioning again.

Is it a god that comes impersonally
in the shape of planes,
or clouds, or horses set like
random dominoes inside a fence?

Or clothed as a man, red-bearded?
brown-skinned? blue-eyed?
Or as a woman,
in the sag of her breasts?
in the curl at her thighs?

Shadows thick as blankets dim our eyes,
engender discontent.

Is it to a god, the dead, or death itself
that we dedicate these monuments?

Nona Everwise, A Close Friend

After solemn words of remembrance,
Harry's body sinks below. The mourners leave
but Nona E., closer to him,
lingers by the grave.

For a dream-like hour she meditates
as shadows lengthen
and assert their evening dominance:

Is it this we live for, only this—
a continuity of generations dead?
a civilization founded on our bones?

Then what is life but singing for the dead?
We whistle in the dark,
and all our art and industry
amount to nothing but a hill of stones.

Yet when we've stood half-hypnotized
before grim mouths of graves,
there's much we must express.
Can we find a melody and keep to it?

I've seen people sing with all their might,
religiously, and nothing came of it.
They spend their lives as I do mine,
assailed by fears and doubts.

That's what we have in common, I suppose:
most of us feel small
when faced with death's stern law,
more inclined to whisper than to shout.

Yet perhaps we could sing with some assurance
that with or without glib promises of heaven,
we all become as children
under the eyelids of our nights;

that we now can reach past far horizons,
letting our sweet and bitter anthems flow,
as everywhere, with swift, consistent rhythms,
dark precisely balances light.

Joel Mobius Remembers Hell

(For my unacknowledged relatives who've been there)
"Nothing burns in hell but the self" —Theologica Germanica

I

Not till the moon's cold craters
bloom with tropical fruits and flowers
will I forget bleak hell.

Hell's close to me
as my pia mater.

Sometimes it attracts me
like a shapely mango,
beckons like a palm tree
gesturing with lush fronds.

It's the father of confession,
the hard mother of compassion,
yet the bringer
of unbelievable anguish.

I'd rather be
a dragonfly in hell
than president of General Motors,
commander of our strongest army,
possessor of an absolute throne.

Hell dominates and teaches
like no man or woman can.
Nor has it equals
among any of the gods.

One could be
a king or queen on earth
and still a fool
in its most elementary level.

II

Hell's our shadows
come alive
and fighting
hard as cornered tigers;

it's an unexplored country
of the mind, an empire
where delusions
are commodities
traded freely;

it's a broken bridge,
flooded isthmus,
drowned peninsula,
cancelled island;

it's every direction:
north, south, east, west,
up, and at all angles—
but, most of all, down.

I could stand
on its tallest peak
and still be in
its lowest depths.

I could swim
in its rivers
and be flying
in its sky.

Those who break
society's strict codes
are dispensed with
by society.

Those who violate
their own taboos
may end in hell.

III

The damned encounter
all things altered
by their vivid ghosts.

In hell
Pandora's box
springs open
and becomes
a thousand boxes
with a million curses
flying out.

All the gruesomeness
of life emerges.

Words may have
as many levels
as great mansions.

Laws of the universe
become erratic
as the flight of bats.

Wisdom may appear
to be incompetence,
compassion, cowardice,
love, redeeming love,
denial of bare truth.

Even stones, trees,
birds and animals may speak
with lucid tongues.

The psyche moves
in total nakedness.

To see oneself
with relentless
inner Xrays—
terrifying!

To lose one's soul
and not know who
or what one is—
excruciating!

IV

Hell's the consciousness
inverted, dirty underwear
worn over outer garb.

The filters of the mind
are useless;
anarchy and chaos reign.

To be a prisoner
of your own split innerness
seems more terrible
than all the tortures
others can devise.

Your mental antibodies
turn against you
like rebelling soldiers.

Confusion is a vulture
that descends to tear
at your defenseless bones.

Yet hell's a holy place,
a site of sacraments
and miracles,
a shrine to the profane.

There you may meet
both gods and devils
in *flagrante dilecto*!

V

Hell's pains
are the agonies
of becoming
rather than accumulating
worldly goods.

It's where humans
ceaselessly transform;
where men are women,
women, men,
each swallowing
their otherness.

It's where either/or
and both/and clash,
producing doubts that torment
like a mad bee swarm.

It's where the new
confronts the old
and one must let go
merely to endure.

Hell excuses nothing.

Each choice seems larger
than the last:
the dead are monitored
with awesome scrupulosity.

Hell allows excessive eating,
but its inhabitants
remain ravenous;

it provides gallons to drink,
which only leads to
more powerful thirsts;

it has congregations
of the incredibly lonely
whom the very touch
of others nauseates.

The moment one grows comfortable,
the landscape alters
like some huge kaleidoscope.

My vision balked
at all the fallen angels!

VI

In hell
exquisite beauty
may engender sadness,
grossness great attraction.

Every soul's a refugee
from being.

Colors may be felt,
textures heard,

random noises
smelled or tasted.

Spells and superstitions
multiply like rabbits
from a black magician's hat.

Symbols rule
with more significance
than human laws.

Prophecy and other gifts
seem possible
and just around
the next blind corner.

Enlightenment
can be a firefly
in deep shadow.

If you want perfection
you can have it,
but the road
leads through your soul.

VII

Hell's shifting boundaries
can't be detected
by the usual five senses.

It's a bitter stream
of consciousness, a river
clashing with a sea
creating ripples, rapids,
whirlpools and reverses.

Yet its geography
is much the same
as earth's—
except for the swift,
incessant changes.

Towns and streets
become labeled
with ambiguous names.

Residences may
seem rife
with rituals,
atrocities,
and assignations.

But don't be misled
by the usual
daymares of the damned.

Hell has neither
three-headed dogs
nor dangerous dragons.

It's internal forces
painfully colliding,
inner conflict so acute
it alters one's universe.

VIII

The underworld
transforms us.

Those who were lions
may come out lambs.

Those who were lamb-like
may emerge as vipers
whipping their split tongues.

There, as in a minefield,
it behooves us
to walk in the footprints
of those who've gone before.

Guides were scarce
but I found one,
my respected friend
and second father,
Doctor Max.

Those who return
like that great man
to heal the damned
make hell's true heroes.

Those others who use
what they know
to torment victims
are death's demons.

(They played
with my psyche
like tigers with
fresh kills,
harassed me
room to room,
neighborhood
to neighborhood.)

When I found a mentor
instead of a torturer,

I discovered an oasis
in an endless,
fearsome wasteland.

IX

Most of hell's inhabitants
have great reverence
for love and life.

They're more sensitive
than the living,
send and receive
more subtle messages.

The damned's alleged tendency
toward violence—
an exaggeration
fed by prejudice.

Some come
to slay mothers
or fathers,
but not in bodily form.

Most are dangerous
only to themselves.

Those star-crossed few
who assault the innocent—
have mercy on them
for they know not
what they do.

But those who kill
and pretend to be hell's victims—
let them penetrate
to the core of screams.

Let them never again see
the blessed ordinary!

X

Hell's free:
it costs nothing to enter
except your unearned soul.

Some innocents choke
on an overdose
of knowledge.

Others expire
from spontaneous combustion.

Though many paths exist
to the underworld,
no one visits
merely as a tourist.

Hell's a passageway,
a birth canal, an initiation
into a sacred fraternity.

It exists
beyond nations,
beyond boundaries,
beyond ethnicities,
and it differs
for each psyche.

If it were stable
and perceivable
to ordinary hacks,
they'd make it a monument,

a plastic park
with guidebooks, souvenirs
and gawkers riding through
in air-conditioned cars.

The damned would hate this
more than death itself.

XI

To go to hell
intentionally,
one has to welcome pain.

For the fortunate
hell's a tunnel
with an opening
at the end.

Remaining there
when an exit's near
and seeking mastery
may work for some;

for others it's futile
as suffering every known ill
to learn how to cure it.
*(Or spread it to friends
and enemies alike!)*

Those people's souls,
like stubborn butterflies,
refuse to light again—

Existence all their lives
in the moon's cold craters
becomes a fearsome possibility,

a cruel milieu
where flaws are magnified
like tiny cracks in diamonds
under a jeweler's powerful glass.

May they salvage what they can
with expert aid,
suture up the rest,
and return to ordinary spaces.

You stunned sufferers,
takers of ultimate pains,
come away
to this familiar world.
Here even ugliness
is much admired!

XII

Hell's acrid fumes,
its flames,
the stench of burning sulfur—
all are myths of the living.

Fire and brimstone
don't exist
except in the self.

Hell's an irregular circle
of great gravity
around each of the dead,
a space to the limits
of their perceptions.

Some, like newborns,
need to suckle
at the breasts of mothers.

A few find fire there;
others, comfort.

Some others must
be consoled
by loving fathers.

Still others need both,
most often in one.

But all, like trembling deer,
sometimes need to be left alone
to run.

Yet be forewarned,
you who'd give favors
and expect great rewards:

the dead are more sensitive
than the living.

Insincerity, to them,
is worse than sin!

XIII

Skeletons appall the living,
but not so much
as do the newly dead
whose hell-crazed eyes
reveal their desperation.

They frighten those
uneasy with their own
closed innerness.

Yet most of the damned
have hope, may even pray

for peace, for a respite
from excessive conflict;

for a harmonious age
when ordinary people
welcome them
as those who've gone beyond,
explorers of
the dark uncommon.

Most return eventually
from anonymity
and institutions,
recognize the virtues
of conventions.

Let the dead
walk among the living
in acceptance
and tranquility.

Let spirits not be broken;
let lives and loves be saved.

XIV

O you noble,
beautiful innocents
who live by simple rules
and take few critical risks,

give up damning prejudice.

If you won't honor the dead,
at least accept them.

Look within and find
the warmth of love,
the sweet balm of compassion.

Follow your kind hearts;
give up your hates.

Let us flourish
in your circles
without anger, fear, regret.

If this world's
too cruel for you,
you can escape;
but the price you must pay,
ah, the price!

If you've courage,
stamina, and faith—
(*Proselytizers will think
I mean religion.*)

If you'd give anything
to be free—

No, I can see
that most of you
are content
with your complaints.

Then, like oysters
with sharp grains of sand inside,
create psychic pearls
to ease your pains.

XV

And you others,
exquisite lords and ladies
who maintain war is peace
as long as you
and yours stay safe—

who control world commodities,
dominate great swaths of earth,
bring gruesome hells to multitudes—

you console yourself
with the most expensive gifts,
endless accoutrements of wealth,
and live for the times
you can forget
the cost of what you've spent.

Your pains are most intense
and the most ignored!

Let's assume you'll remain
in the stifling cage
of more! more! more!

Some night soon
you'll dream of a day
shiny as a bright new limousine.

The sun will rise
like molten gold
and flood the peaks with light.

The rivers and lakes
will gleam like platinum.

You hope someday to own it all
but have a hunger
equal to your greed.
*(That you read this poem,
is proof enough!)*

Be good to the damned
lest you wake
condemned to pay
in their expensive currency.

Acknowledgments

The following poems first appeared, some in different versions, in the chapbook *A Confluence of Voices* (Finishing Line Press, 2011): "Tom Tenderfoot," "Goliath Speaks," "Dana B. Fawn," "Petra Possible, Survivor," "Annett Loveless," "Corporal Tim Washington," "Herb Mindfree, M.D.," "Quincy Collander," "Harvey Stonecypher," "Grandma May Amoro," "H. Howard Hexagon," "Jack Root," "Robert Bitterroot," "Randy Woods," "J. P. Grady," "Don J. Duquesne," "Juan Martinez, Orchardist," "Dale Tryst," "Professor Peavy and the Motorcyclists," "Jonathon Northcutt, Able Seaman," "Peter Paul Persimian," "Beth Duncan," and "Sam Slipper, Schizophrenic."

Versions of these poems were first published in the chapbook *Colma* (Futurecycle Press, 2007): "Blake Reservoir, The Passing," "Phillip Diamondcutter, Embalmer," "Fred Wallenstone, Mason," "Arthur Scarbird, Philosopher," "Jose Tremelo, Musician," "Lynnette Purplethorn, Clergy," and "Nona Everwise, A Close Friend."

About FutureCycle Press

FutureCycle Press is dedicated to publishing lasting English-language poetry books, chapbooks, and anthologies in both print-on-demand and Kindle ebook formats. Founded in 2007 by long-time independent editor/publishers and partners Diane Kistner and Robert S. King, the press incorporated as a nonprofit in 2012. A number of our editors are distinguished poets and writers in their own right, and we have been actively involved in the small press movement going back to the early seventies.

The FutureCycle Poetry Book Prize and honorarium is awarded annually for the best full-length volume of poetry we publish in a calendar year. Introduced in 2013, our Good Works projects are anthologies devoted to issues of universal significance, with all proceeds donated to a related worthy cause. Our Selected Poems series highlights contemporary poets with a substantial body of work to their credit; with this series we strive to resurrect work that has had limited distribution and is now out of print.

We are dedicated to giving all of the authors we publish the care their work deserves, making our catalog of titles the most diverse and distinguished it can be, and paying forward any earnings to fund more great books.

We've learned a few things about independent publishing over the years. We've also evolved a unique, resilient publishing model that allows us to focus mainly on vetting and preserving for posterity poetry collections of exceptional quality without becoming overwhelmed with bookkeeping and mailing, fundraising activities, or taxing editorial and production "bubbles." To find out more about what we are doing, come see us at www.futurecycle.org.

The FutureCycle Poetry Book Prize

All full-length volumes of poetry published by FutureCycle Press in a calendar year are considered for the annual FutureCycle Poetry Book Prize. This allows us to consider each submission on its own merits, outside of the context of a contest. Too, the judges see the finished book, which will have benefitted from the beautiful book design and strong editorial gloss we are famous for.

The book ranked the best in judging is announced as the prize-winner in the subsequent year. There is no fixed monetary award; instead, the winning poet receives an honorarium of 20% of the total net royalties from all poetry books and chapbooks the press sold online in the year the winning book was published. The winner is also accorded the honor of being on the panel of judges for the next year's competition; all judges receive copies of all contending books to keep for their personal library.